UNRAVELING

Natasha Patel

First Published in February 2021

ISBN: 978-93-5427-498-5

BLUEROSE PUBLISHERS

www.bluerosepublishers.com

info@bluerosepublishers.com

+91 8882 898 898

Cover Design:

Riya Parkar

Typographic Design:

Tanya Raj Upadhyay

Distributed by: BlueRose, Amazon, Flipkart, Shopclues

BOOK REVIEW

DR. VINOD KUMAR GOYAL
MBBS

Unraveling is Natasha's first book, which is majorly streamed on her personal experiences based on psychoanalysis therefore psychodynamics which was supported by me. In this book she clearly puts on paper what matters to commonly other people at this age; keeping the past in the past, and understanding detachment is one of them. Giving up on the past, and all that was valued is a journey many people at this age pschogically go through which majorly affects their aim, purpose, and mission in life. In my opinion, this book or her understanding will help many people to get a better meaning to their pain and suffering. I appreciate her interest in making a difference, which is an inspirational model for all those people willing to help others.

To everyone who laughs a little while reading, and understands my underrated humour.

To the people who were my sudden jolt of panic and motivation.

To that one hoodie which I referenced a lot, Rest In Peace.

AGENDA

CHAPTER ONE

THE BEGINNING: THE PAIN

Pain. I believe it to be a crucial part of life without which you wouldn't have turned to pursue this book for help nor would I have had to compose it. It is because of those whammies in life that cause us pain that we are built the way we are and constantly metamorphose to the way we should be. That whammy being life itself. Before you move ahead with any false expectations let me make something clear. I am not writing this book to end your pain, because let's face it, not even a Panadol can end all pain. I am writing this because I want you to understand why you're suffering and enduring this pain. Not to evanesce this pain, but to understand why you and I are suffering because of this pain. Someone once told me in order to perceive one, we must recognise what hinders them and what saddens their heart because that is what illustrates matters they truly value. I believe that this thought is the stepping stone for you and me now, to recall our past where this thought becomes a question: what is it I valued that now causes me suffering? So, now we start this journey where we look back to the pages where it all began: the moment we faced loss. No matter how much you attempted to hold on, they or it slipped away like trickles of rain against your palm, right? Something that you depended on, something that had emotionally weaved its path toward you, now lost. You can feel each nerve down to your feet, grieving for this loss. This is the kind of pain you and I feel, and so do the others who grieve for their loss. But it is not all that sappy, and I will not continue to coddle you or myself with all that "I can feel you, I really understand." I won't continue to do so because I really do understand, and all that toxic positivity and honey-coated words are not something that you need. So I do understand you. However, the big guy in this game is something that none of us truly understand and it is the realm you have created inside of you.

This, the loss you're going through isn't something that you *have* to fight, but instead something you are willingly opting for. A challenge against yourself for yourself. Right now you are in a position I barely know anything about, but I do know how it feels to be hurt and holding on. Regardless of whether it is you that let go of your end of the string or them. It presumably could be an object too, which was perhaps lost or stolen, a piece you considered to be your strength, like a piece of you, now gone. You are hurting, and hurt is still one of the most beautiful, gut-wrenching, and worthwhile things I have lived to witness and encounter. What's more, in spite of what you experience today it will someday be one of the most valuable experiences of your life. But again that's not what I am here to say. I am here to tell you that pain and suffering are hard, it is something all of us go through, every single day. You merely have to live with it, by embracing it.

No matter how the object or person was taken away from you, you have the right to grieve. Grieving does not mean you're weak, nor is it a remembrance of everything that's gone, but a mere tale of something or someone truly valued. And it is a process. Allowing yourself to grieve is an important step along the way, side-by-side with acceptance and realisation of independence. Do not be too harsh on yourself like I was, constantly striking myself down when I felt the pain, when I felt like crying my heart out or when I wanted to scream at the top of my lungs for help. Do it, who's stopping you? When you realise you've been doing that for long, it will be too late, you might have already hammered the nail down. Don't, don't be an idiot like I was. A loss at the end of the day is a loss, it cannot be compared or equalled to someone else's, what you're going through is not lesser or greater than anyone else's pain. It might be different when it comes to suffering. How much it is rending you apart right now, it once did for me too and someday it will be the same for someone else. This is the circle of life. Just like the moon goes from waxing to waning, just like it has its different phases, so do we, loss just happens to be one of them. A pretty huge and painful phase of life. It is vital and frequent, whether it be when you were five and had to let go of your favourite toy or whether it is you now letting go of your favourite person. It holds such value because it moulds for us the key to the next phase. The key you shape right now is a form of you after a process of metamorphosis, more grounded and mature. And again as the new phase awakens, you fight by yourself with your own materials and potentials, and transform yet again. You see, we are like nomads, or at least we have to be – to transform is to live.

If you were the one that let them or it go, you must have had reasons. If it was the opposite, they must have had reasons. You lost something, the universe must have had ample reasons. It is for the best in the long run to have the courage to let yourself fall and shatter and to be strong enough to piece yourself back again, but firmer this time. And to be a tougher version of yourself, you'll have to progress through phases, dozens of them. This, where you're at right now, is an early phase where you indulge yourself in a generous amount of self-pity for the loss, unaware that you will have to walk away from it one definite day. Unaware that even though you're hurting and have to face the reality, not everything can be about you. And for that one definite day to come, when you realise that not everything is unicorns and sparkles, you will have to put your all to and for yourself. The possibility of this day to come solemnly lies in you, and the *choices you are minded to make*.

One element that has always taken me by surprise is how much one does not know about themselves, how much I remain a mystery to myself. This process is an opening for you to get to know what truly matters to you. Distinguishing who you are and what you stand for are one of the most essential things one has to do in life, and yes, it is considered to be the most arduous because it then decides our path of suffering. But again, no pain no gain, baby. It's a process, not just a matter of a few seconds or days. Some people take a lifetime to do it (or a few months that feel like a lifetime) and others take less than that, oh how I envy them. However, there is no solid version of who you really are, as times come situations change and so do people. In an environment that constantly changes, we cannot expect ourselves to remain the same, thus making adaptation and transformation inevitable and essential. And here too, you have a choice in what sort of transformation you aspire. Doors will invariably be revealed, you either take it or leave it, that's on you. *The Beginning: The Pain* is all about first coming to terms with the fact that whatever you're going through right now, the experience, is not bad. I know the situation does not favour you, but that does not mean it's bad for you. The term 'bad' is almost always associated with something negative, while in fact, it is the complete opposite. Why is a negative experience bad for you? Because it hurts you? Have we now become so full of ourselves that we cannot identify the value of this pain? I'll answer that for you, yes we have and also we always were. When you pass it all, you'll look back and be proud of the storm you weathered with how much it hurt every giving second. What you will also have is a better version of yourself. So, technically the process is not bad but concrete in the long run. You need to realise that without any negatives in our life, we would practically not be alive. Without Walt Disney being demoralised by his editor nothing would have provoked him to give the best our children see today. Without failing multiple times, I wouldn't have been able to write this chapter. Negativity has the power to change things, it has the power to change our thoughts into action. If the voices in your head never made you feel bad about yourself, you would be 70 percent ice cream and still be looking for a good show on Netflix. Without that kind of self-actualisation, we would still be living on square one.

So, acknowledge that this situation and the way you wield it affects the foundation for the time interval between this fall until your next. The effortless dismissal of 'negative' thoughts has reaped over the world, which for me is a fallacy. Because of this, our minds have evolved to hopelessly moving forward, without evaluating our errors in history. I, instead, tend to scrutinise and explore our falsities because I stand by the opinion that our thoughts have so much more weight to them than we already know of. And one can only get to know their thoughts better when they get to know *the realm they have created inside of themselves; their mind.* So, we move on with the chapters hoping and trying to do so.

WHAT I GOT FROM THIS CHAPTER

CHAPTER TWO

WHY

Why are you hurt? Why do you cry endless hours every night because of this loss? Why are you suffering? Simply because you care. What you care about clearly reflects the priorities you have set for yourself. And this is what you decided to care about. As a child, I only cared about my Beyblades and stuffed animals, so every time I would break or lose one, I bawled my eyes out. Now that I'm older, I still manage to do the same, because I choose to do so. I still care about every damn thing that seems to exist, because I make myself believe it is of value to me. Clearly, I haven't very well adapted to change, and the fact that I simply cannot control everything that goes on around me, and thus, I suffer and hurt myself. As do you. As we grow older our priorities change and become more distinct to us, and yes, not everyone must have developed to do so, there still might be people who cry when their ice cream falls. Because they care, and because they simply choose to care. Pain is something that comes to all, it is predestined, but suffering is something that you can control, something you pick. However, generally, our priorities change from being "I should be next on the slide" to "I should be doing this to make my CV look better", and that's called being mature, which clearly you and I are still building towards. It's a long process, at the end of which you simply start caring solemnly about the things that are actually worth fighting for, something that makes pain easier for you because you chose it. And whether you are wholly ready for suffering is on you to decide. With this kind of maturity also comes the understanding that nothing in this world is permanent. You will lose all that you have today, someday; just like you were born empty-handed, you will die that way too.

This way of thinking and acceptance that all you can control is yourself makes letting go easier. And when you understand the only thing you can control truly is yourself and your actions, you will realise you are going through this phase of suffering because you decided to care about it, whether it be the object, the situation, or the person; you made yourself believe that it is something worth fighting for. And now you're here, hopefully over the phase of self-pity, here to face the reality that you chose this for yourself and now you probably regret it and well obviously you've got some work to do there, buddy.

When you decided to care about your favourite hoodie, you also subsequently accepted the pain you'd go through when you would lose it. Through the phase since you first got it, to the day you lost it, you have built an emotional path towards it, something called attachment. Something that you consider to be of importance in your day to day life. The strong sensation of belongingness; a sense of authority that we assemble. Though the idea of attachment sounds like the best thing you could have, that homely feeling of being needed by someone and even though it is exactly the kind of love you crave, it's not pure love. Because then, they would not just accept you, but also call you out when you're wrong. They will not be afraid to tell you you're at fault because they simply want you to grow, that's how I see it. Love isn't only about the sugar-coated words, but about how the other person in the relationship is willing to show you the harsh reality and still support you. The people I have loved the most in my life have told me that if work is the only thing I will ever prioritise, I'll start losing everyone. When I first heard that, very obviously I was soul-shattered, but they said it and that's what matters to me. They weren't scared that if they say something wrong and upsetting, I'll leave them. That is what I consider to be pure love. You would either agree with me or disagree or maybe if you're indecisive you'll agree and disagree. But again, what is pure for everyone, right? I perceive that to be a question that cannot be answered until your dying breath. Until parts of your life, that you have truly, purely loved are reflected back to you. The reminiscences I get of *Kimi No Na Wa* on my deathbed is and will be pure love. For which I believe in this situation, if it were to be pure and real love, it would've been way easier to let go of it or them in a way, right? The idea of a truly loved one leaving you for their happiness and alleviation wouldn't have been so tough, would it? (Until the case here is completely different, which again I do not know about) The acceptance would've come along easier than it is right now. You would be satisfied and fulfilled just knowing they are happy now, with or without you, whereas attachment is the opposite. Even though you may be happy for them, you are still upset because you're not as important a part of their life as you were before, and yes, that sucks but we often overlook the fact that they/it is in a happier environment now.

Attachment for me is more of a selfish love whereas love is meant to be selfless, there is a fine line between the two, nonetheless love as a component majorly incorporates attachment. But a bond of attachment does not cross its boundaries. Attachment and love are two things that we never quite see coming, and well they go hand-in-hand. Almost every day I communicated with my friend who liked the Scorpions as much as I did, it soon came to me that it was quite impossible to go a day without talking to them, thus coming to the realisation that I had built an attachment, pretty normal after you talk every day, right? That was my full stop, until one day out of the blue I realised that I loved them while they taught me how to cut lemons! It honestly seemed like the most obnoxious thing at first, falling for my best friend, but I never saw it coming. Whereas, to my roommate, whom I loved from the beginning, even when we talked barely twice a day, I formed my attachment almost a year after. After a whole year of rib cage pain, thank you for that by the way. For me attachment has always seemed to come before love, because of the fear I have of the word 'love', the immense responsibility that comes after scares me, but again slowly my feelings catch up to the word, and I come to that one day when I have to admit it. I tried running away from writing this too, but again I had to. For others it can be different, you love someone and then you form an attachment to them, like me and my WWE champion roommate. Either way, love and attachment always work together, as a balanced equation. It is a crucial part of love, but when this attachment gradually starts to transform into a bond more substantial it turns volatile and fragile subsequently. We were born detached, unaware, and unlinked to any in this world, as we grew older we formed attachments in our primary relationships, because of love. It is something we learned and adapted to which then guided our way of attachment in other relationships. The very first attachment theorist John Bowlby stated attachment to be "[a] lasting psychological connectedness between human beings." Bowlby explains the process of attachment throughout our life in his theory. About how an infant first develops an attachment purely based on their needs to their caretaker. For me, that is something we still do. The attachment for the constant need to be felt accepted and placid with ourselves. When we were mere infants and didn't get what we needed, we cried. Some still do the same. That is an unhealthy attachment because feeling accepted and loved by others is not a need, but a want we take to be our need.

So how do we identify what is healthy and unhealthy attachment? Bowlby's theory also states that every different person builds their own way of attachment given their backgrounds. To which I agree, today what you are going through might not have been something others have gone through yet, you build different approaches to attachment now that you are more aware of what certain unhealthy attachments might lead up to, whereas a child does not. So, here are the two ways dominance comes along:

1. In a relationship, togetherness as well as solitary are important. However much you are a team, equally, you are two different people. The missing of this recognition of solitary; the incompetence to be able to stand up by oneself is toxic. One comes alone into this world and exits alone too. When you start depending on the other person, you lose your independence. This can also be applied to the cases of attachments towards materialistic items. I, for example, have seen people get attached to items they call lucky, hell, I do the same. Instead of studying for the chemistry test, I take my lucky pen, cause that'll totally answer the questions right. And when we lose that lucky pen we think we'll fail every test, well for one if you don't study,

you surely will. But it is that complete dependency we have built on the pen, that we forget it is our responsibility to actually read the notes for the test.

2. When you start giving up things that mattered the most to you for them and their feelings. You have worked all your life to get your dream job and now that you finally have it, you're happy. However, if your significant other isn't very pleased with that, do you quit? If you do just because you fear losing them, that's an unhealthy attachment. I myself have given up on things I loved to do just because of the fear of losing them, look what happened, I lost them anyway. And I lost the thing I loved to do too, and that is what I regret. Surely, there are people who would be happy to give up their job to make it comfortable for others. But as a Robin Scherbatsky myself or at least what my friends believe me to be, I would say if they really loved you, they wouldn't ask you to give up something so important to you, I wouldn't at least. Well perhaps if it did come to Harry Styles I would understand.

3. When you make your life theirs. This situation is kind of like a plumber uncalled for. Whenever a pipe breaks at my house, I am responsible for fixing it, it's my life. I can surely ask them how to, but I cannot let them. Don't be like our dear Jane Villanueva and meddle. Forsaking everything you're doing and going to "help" the other person without letting them know, is clearly an invasion of privacy. And we all know what is a relationship without respect for privacy. There are some things that have to be fought by one themselves, it cannot

be solved by the help or interference of others. Such as the process of letting go. It sure is your independent journey, people can come and advise you, but it's upon you to take the advice and apply it. When you constantly want to or actually do it, it's an unhealthy attachment. This is also called 'Rescue Behaviour' because you cannot see them struggle and thus try and "rescue" them without even the minute awareness that you're creating a dent in your own relationship.

These are the three most common ways, but evidently, there might be more things that certify as an unhealthy attachment to you and me. So now we're aware, at least I am, that we have built an attachment to the thing or person we're trying to let go of, and it's hard because with attachment comes the trust that they'll always be there. Which isn't the reality now, is it? Everything that comes, goes.

WHAT I GOT FROM THIS CHAPTER

CHAPTER THREE

YOU'RE WRONG… ACCORDING TO ME

If we are aware that all that comes eventually goes, why do we still get attached to materialistic and non-materialistic things? Because we then know that it belongs to us, it is something or someone that is in our hands to control. And when we start losing control of things and people around us, it feels as though everything is falling apart and we're helpless. We seem to despise that, the sensation of things falling apart because it makes us feel low and unworthy. Whereas we're constantly loved, accepted, and authorised when we are around that object or person. We feel good about ourselves and we feel as though we have a permit to do anything and they'll always be there, loving us. It is that what we have lost and now we're grieving for; the way we wanted to feel wanted, the way we've always wanted to feel supreme and accepted.

Why? Ask yourself, why was it so important for you to feel appreciated, supreme, and accepted? Because you and I, like everyone else, are entitled to feel that way. The more constantly we are being appreciated and coddled with their love and mere intimate existence, the more dominant we seem to become unconsciously. Our unconscious mind automatically builds up an ideology about us always being correct, and everyone on the opposition being wrong, so we never learn. The constant support from the people around to whom you're attached to, or to whose way of acceptance you're attached to makes you feel this dominance. This dominance is then what guides your behaviours toward other people. There are two main ways this behaviour is portrayed in situations. It is this situation of letting go too.

1. Portrayed narcissism: This is something that people around you can see when you think you're the only one who'll ever really feel this pain. As if no one understands you, you're a special bud with special problems. Trust me, not even God has that kind of time to spare, to give you special problems of your own. You're just like everyone else, you face the very problems a human does in their circle of life. So, you're not special, in fact you're just another average person going through average life problems and finding difficulties solving them. Now knowing this you should really stop being arrogant to those around you, they do understand how hard it is to get over a loss, and even if they do not, one day they certainly will.

2. Self-victimisation: "I don't deserve them, they're too good for a person like me. That's why they left me." Tell me your first response to this wouldn't be "No man, you are more than what they think. It's their loss anyway." All those sugar-coated words make me want to slam people's faces with reality, the brutal reality. In fact, it was just yesterday that I heard one of my friends say that exact same thing, and I really had nothing sugar-coated ready for them. I told them that victimising yourself is equally entitled to those who think they're too good for any of us. Through self-victimisation, the dominance comes gradually, like slow poison, for you and the people around you. I never considered this to be bad. In fact, this is what I always did, until one day I realised how distant I had become

> from the real world as my friend told me she was facing the very problem I had which I didn't tell anyone about because I thought no one would ever be able to understand me and feel that way. That instant was a big "The joke's on you!" and that's all I could think about at that time. I'm sorry friend for making you repeat what you said.

If you noticed meticulously, both of these ways have something in common: the thought that no one will ever be able to comprehend and relate to what you're saying or feeling. The unique snowflake feeling, all that crap. The certainty that you're special is what stops you from maturing and communicating. We never consider actually going up to some acquaintance and talking about our loss because of the fear of what they might think, what they might perceive us to be, life's too short to think about anything like that. In fact, I dare to do that right now. Now you see what builds up the certainty – you. You make yourself believe that you're so right and can never be wrong about anything, so you can already declare what others *might* think. There was this one school team that I had put all my efforts into for that year, yet I was so certain that I would never be able to make it on the team, a thought I considered to be my future reality. Because of that certainty, the one my stupid brain made up, I was obstructed from sending an email saying that I was interested in joining their team for the competition. But guess what, they took everyone who responded despite their qualification. That regret is a tough one to let go of for me, all caused by something I considered would happen for sure. Mark Manson states "Certainty is the enemy of growth", which I believe to be true. How many misconceptions you make in your mind is how high your barrier will be between you and seeking a whole new perspective. A perspective that allows us, humans, to know that at the end of the day we're all like, yet choose to be so different. Being unaware that the passion to doubt is necessary for our lives. "I have studied over five hours for the test, I should get all the answers correct." That is one certainty I've heard over a million times, and in the end whoever I heard it from ended up passing by a fluke, including me. Building up certainties about the future in your life is as good as setting expectations. In the end of which nothing ever goes right, nor will it ever go right. Because you were so certain about something or someone's actions, you prepared yourself for it, while you never prepared yourself for the complete opposite of that happening. That's why being completely open to the possibility of anything happening is important. And that, my friend, is what life will serve you, every day, something new completely out of the blue. If you predicted something like that and were prepared, which is very rare, good for you. But if you didn't, now you'll waste most of your time thinking and brooding about how you're so unlucky.

As mentioned before, you either blame it all on yourself, or on the people and situations around you, from which none does any good to you. They just assure you that you're right no matter what the situation is. You're the one that has to be treated specially because what happened to you was wrong. If they left you, you're still right, completely ignoring all the bad you've done that made them leave. If you left them, you're still right, because the relationship became toxic, and you have to get your mental peace. If something materialistic was lost, inevitably, we become right because it cannot feel pain, only we go through pain, so we're right. What if I say you're wrong about thinking you're right? Inarguably your reaction would be "Maybe I am" or "What do you even know about me?" I do know that both of those ways are domination, and I also know that through both these ways you are trying to simply prove that you're right. Through one, you're looking for external sympathy, for people to pity you, and through the other you're merely being straightforwardly disdainful. The thinking of us always being right is something we have learned over the years, a habit we have built up through our daily choices. Why did I choose not to apologise to my sister because I was so certain that I was right? And when my parents backed me up, it boosted my ego to not apologise the next time too when it would completely be my fault. Why are we upset because of this loss right now? Because clearly, it did not go the way we wanted it to, something we were so certain about. But somehow we still manage to find the ways that make us seem right, always and that's human nature. But one thing to understand here is what is right for me, will possibly never be right for someone else. So yes, you are right...from your point of view. And yes, you're also wrong...from my point of view. Domination is just a way of changing that, changing my opinion to make me believe you're right through self-pity or arrogance. Because we as humans always tend to play this game when we let go: 'Who's at fault?' and pretty obviously we want to be the victims of the situation. So we dominate.

When you're certain about something or someone, you're holding on to it, you purposefully aren't letting go of it because you think you're right. And to be suffering means to be holding on.

WHAT I GOT FROM THIS CHAPTER

CHAPTER FOUR

THERE'S YOU AND THEN THERE'S ME

A continuum if I were to say, from the dominant actions to cognisance. I know the suffering hasn't all gone, it still hurts and it always will, what matters is how you deal with it. The way you choose to deal with this loss affects your life in the long run. Being a human you'll always be pulled towards things that will offer you immediate gratification; a short-term happiness roller-coaster or in simple words: a distraction. A short-term happiness roller-coaster is easily available, anywhere you go, whatever you are going through because we make it open for ourselves. Buying everything off of Amazon or drinking any amount of alcohol isn't going to get you to forget how you feel, trust me if it did, I would've emptied my father's bank account and would be sniffing sharpies. It numbs you for a short time until you're hit harder with reality someday. What it will do is push your problems so deep, that they eventually become your unconsciously driving emotions. Those emotions that could have costed me bankruptcy will now guide my life without me even knowing. You lose all control over something you could once handle. And when that happens the id part of your personality has successfully played a bigger role in the equation of ego. Id is the component of your unconscious personality that drives your needs and wants, your pleasures and satisfactions. Reaching out for water after a run is a need, wanting to eat more chocolates after you just had dinner at 2 am is a want that we consider to be a need, which is something I need to understand too after stuffing twenty wrappers in my paint box, sorry Mom! On the contrary, there is our superego which is the 'home of legislation' for us, the component reflecting our morality and values. Superego is somewhat like our protective barrier. I shouldn't sneak out of the house to go to a party, why? Because that disobeys my value of being honest towards the people around me. This raises a question about our ego, what is it? The equal balance of my id and superego is my ego; how much I am able to differentiate and balance my prerequisite needs with my fantasising desires. It is basically how much I can stretch toward the sky with my feet still intact on earth. And just how the balance works for me (well, it might be a tad bit unstable now but I'm getting there), it is for you and for everyone else.

There are two paths you can take to handle the situation right now, either you go for temporary highs or you simply don't. The choice is yours; or should I say your ego's. Are you letting your id win? Or are you instead willing to take the path better in the long run? There is no correct answer, everyone has their right to pick the way they want to walk towards. Whether they want to repeat positive cliché chants all day or actually get up and examine what might be the problem. We all have done that before, haven't we, gotten up the morning after morning, stood in front of the mirror, and told ourselves lies. "Today will be the day I will be happy", and the next moment they're angry because someone finished their strawberry cornflakes and now they can't be happy, true story by the way. So often we have realised that to be happy we have to make our surroundings more comfortable, but can a diffused bulb make its surroundings bright? The actual underlying problem here is you. The way you think. The way you make yourself think. Life will never be comforting. Never. The question is why are you so scared to face reality and find temporary escapes? Id is the answer, your comfort zone. We find comfort in escaping, us humans always find comfort in running away from our problems. Believe me, as I write I remember all the times I have run away from my problems and eventually been chased until I faced a bigger pain than that I would've. As I have mentioned earlier in Chapter I, here fighting isn't external, but internal. How much I've run away from the fact that I will have to face my honest feelings while writing this book, makes me realise I've been doing it all wrong. Blaming others. Self-victimising. Sometimes both. Just finding some way or the other to try and dominate those around me. Why? Because I was afraid to look myself in the eye, and accept that it is me who has caused so much suffering to myself. Blaming others and self-pitying was my escape until I finally realised I was doing nothing but taking a hammer and pinning myself down for more self-destruction.

Temporary high is a type of self-destruction that is quite often obvious to the third-person. They are usually compulsive addictions like shopping, gaming, or drugs. Whereas there are certain things we do on a regular basis, where we unknowingly sabotage ourselves. These are called maladaptive behaviours, procrastination happens to be one of them. Something that you and I have written down in our minds to be our mundane, I was supposed to be working on this chapter yesterday, but here I am. These behaviours are the barriers that often keep us from adapting and growing after a loss. Maladaptive behaviours are like the hidden part of the iceberg. I do know that I procrastinate (a LOT), but also I have no idea what I am trying to avoid. Which is now certain – something I find to be difficult for myself to accomplish. Something that puts me in a position where I feel stupid. I procrastinated this because I would have to research and write and rephrase sentences until they sounded right and honestly, to an extent it made sense; which made me feel stupid. So, I procrastinated, everything then became out of control for me including my visions for the rest of this book. Clearly, nothing seemed to push me anymore, so there was no action. There was no action toward something that had been troubling me unconsciously. But now that I come to realise this at 3:00 am in the morning fuelled up on black coffee, nothing can stop me from typing. From one thought to another. For a hot minute, I was in a phase of self-destruction. Just like how I was before, self-victimising myself for someone I let go of. It's a pattern. However, the most harmful if I were to say, is maladaptive daydreaming, the state of mind that deeply builds upon our "what-ifs".

What if I hadn't removed my favourite, limited edition hoodie that day? I would've still had it and could've worn it to so many places. What if I gave that person one more chance? What if they really changed? Maybe if I just asked that person how they were doing one time, they would've known I still care. Maybe. These are the heart-sinking and honestly dull-witted questions that run through my head. What are yours? When you think of some, you'll realise they often reflect the regrets you have. Things you wanted to do, but did not, things you didn't want to do, but you did. Such as, removing the hoodie and keeping it in a field full of people who had the same one is my regret, seriously how dumb could've I been to do that? Or it could be a pang of guilt. What if I hadn't eaten my sister's chocolate bar? She and I would've survived just one day without fighting. It's in us humans to overthink and destroy what we have done and obsess over something we haven't. This is what maladaptive daydreams are about. You and I both repeatedly live in this fantasy world of ours where we make up situations that favour us, with no idea how much we are dismantling ourselves. By doing this, we are constantly distancing ourselves from reality. We are making it harder for ourselves to accept what's happening around us, the situations that do not favour us, the hard situations. That is our common ground.

WHAT I GOT FROM THIS CHAPTER

CHAPTER FIVE

"YOU CHOSE POORLY"

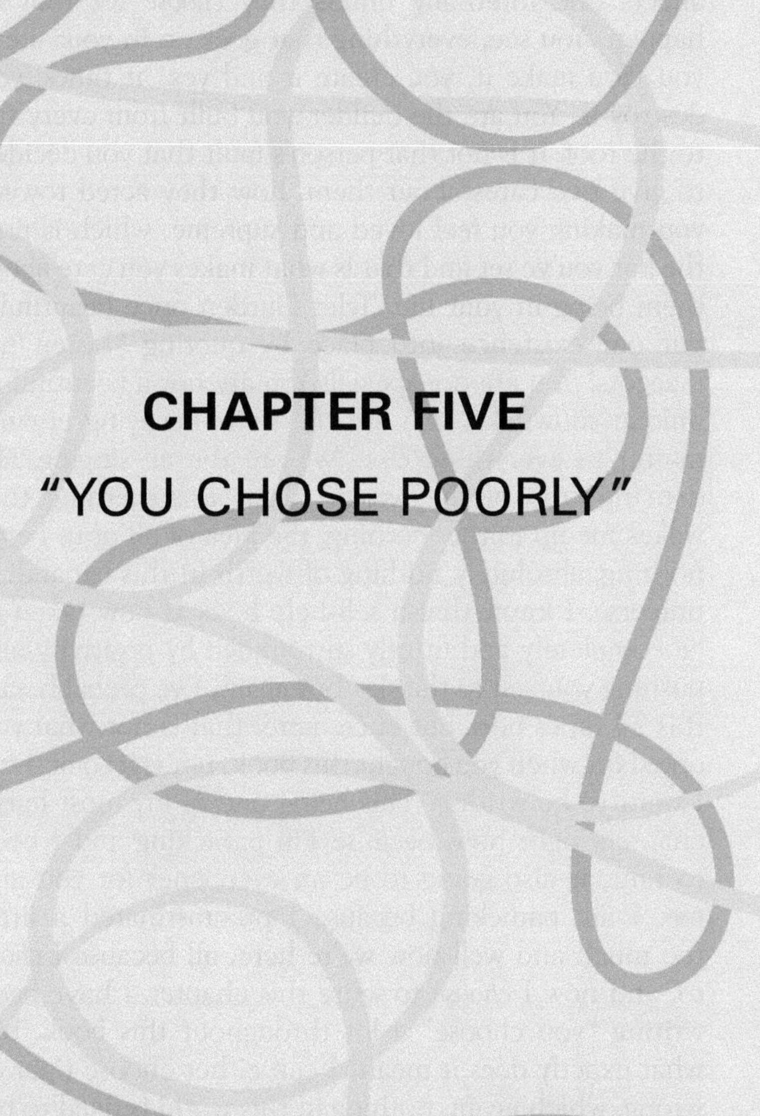

What exactly is it that we are trying to let go of? The thing that is supposedly hurting us or the thing we are making up to hurt ourselves? Nothing that is done externally affects one internally unless they *choose* for that to happen. You see, everything that goes on in your life is you. You make it, you create it and yes, at times, you destroy it. You are the builder, you built from every tile to the roof. It is not that person's fault that you decided to give two cares about them, how they acted toward you making you feel loved and supreme, which is now the bar you've set and that is what makes you care about them being in your life. Tyler Durden once beautifully put our existence into place by quoting "Listen up, maggots! You are not special. You are not a beautiful or unique snowflake. You are the same decaying organic matter as everything else. We are the all-singing, all-dancing crap of the world." That is something that wakes me up in the morning, the idea of all of us being nothing, absolutely nothing of worth in this expanding universe. I know that a self-help book is now taken to be completely and utterly surrounded by positivity and pushing yourself to the sky. But again, I've probably said this 20 times now, but once more: that is not what you opted for when you bought this book, nor is it something I want to be writing. This being one of my most harsh chapters right now, because I'm panicking and I need to rant, is also going to be an eyeopener for you and me. I am panicking because I procrastinated a little too much and well now we're here, all because I *chose* to, and now I *choose* to write this chapter. I have been writing "you choose" a lot throughout this book, but what exactly does it mean? I can either choose right or wrong, which again, nothing in this world is fixed to be.

What something I think is right, for someone else may not be. My right answer to that question can be "you choose", which means you're responsible for it, but for someone else, my answer could be one that can send me to hell. For you, letting go of someone because it causes you pain would be sinful, once it was for me too. But as we grow, with more experience, things eventually start to change and become more clear to you. Not that I'm a wise old owl here telling you all the secrets to life. But I will tell you with the 15 years of experience I've had, what someone or something does never affects you until you *choose* for it to. The pain will inevitably come, but from what and where is on you. For that to be understood, you need to ask yourself, what is it that you want and what is it that you do not want? Those are some very difficult questions, I know. But without putting yourself into doubt, without putting yourself into a spot where you have to undoubtedly question yourself and be made uncomfortable, you'll never be able to know the truth about yourself. Which at the end of the day, doesn't affect me but you and only you. Without putting myself into a position where I questioned my choices and feelings, I would've never been writing this book with all the will I have. Because I know what I consider to be right for me.

You right now are choosing to let go of the pain the past has caused you, why? Because it hurts holding on, doesn't it? Why does it hurt? Because they or it made us feel special, prioritised, and loved. That is what you have lost, so what is it that you are holding on to?

The hope of them or it coming back to you. The fact that you are right and they are wrong, and they will have to come back to you. That is what you're holding on to. Even the slightest hope of them coming back, because now you don't feel loved and prioritised, and you think that you need to feel that way. NO. That is the art of accepting yourself. The art that allows you to take control of yourself, rather than trying to control things that you simply cannot. You can never expect life to treat you all good because that simply is not possible. You will not feel loved, prioritised, and special every given minute. At least not externally. I do not want another sunny day here, is it possible for me to fly up to the sky and hide the sun in any way? No. What I can do is bathe in a tub of ice-cream so I do not feel hot, that is something I can control. Actually, my mom wouldn't allow that. But it is my choice. When we truly understand this, what we are going through isn't suffering anymore. However you might be in pain, it's something that doesn't go away. But suffering does, with the understanding that I did this and now it is in my hands to undo it, to unravel it. What you understand is that this is the good suffering you are going through to reach your goal, a goal you chose. I was personally questioned many times that if I am suffering because of putting my all into my studies, then why don't I just lay back and chill? Because I simply cannot. I once faced the same doubt, that if it's making me stay up late and look like a goth with the darkest shade of eyeshadow possible then why am I doing this? It came to my realisation that this is something I am willing to struggle for, something that at the end of the day, after draining me so much, still manages to motivate me. Why? Because of that one day; that one day which I am willing to work towards. What is that one day for you? What are you mentally prepared to fight for? And that's what makes this an important phase in the process of letting go. The phase that makes you come to a point of self-actualisation that all happens because I let it happen. Now, either you learned that yes, this is the thing I am willing to struggle for or you learned that I shouldn't have cared so much about this thing or person. Perhaps, this learning will give you enough wisdom to know what to do when you are finally able to move on.

WHAT I GOT FROM THIS CHAPTER

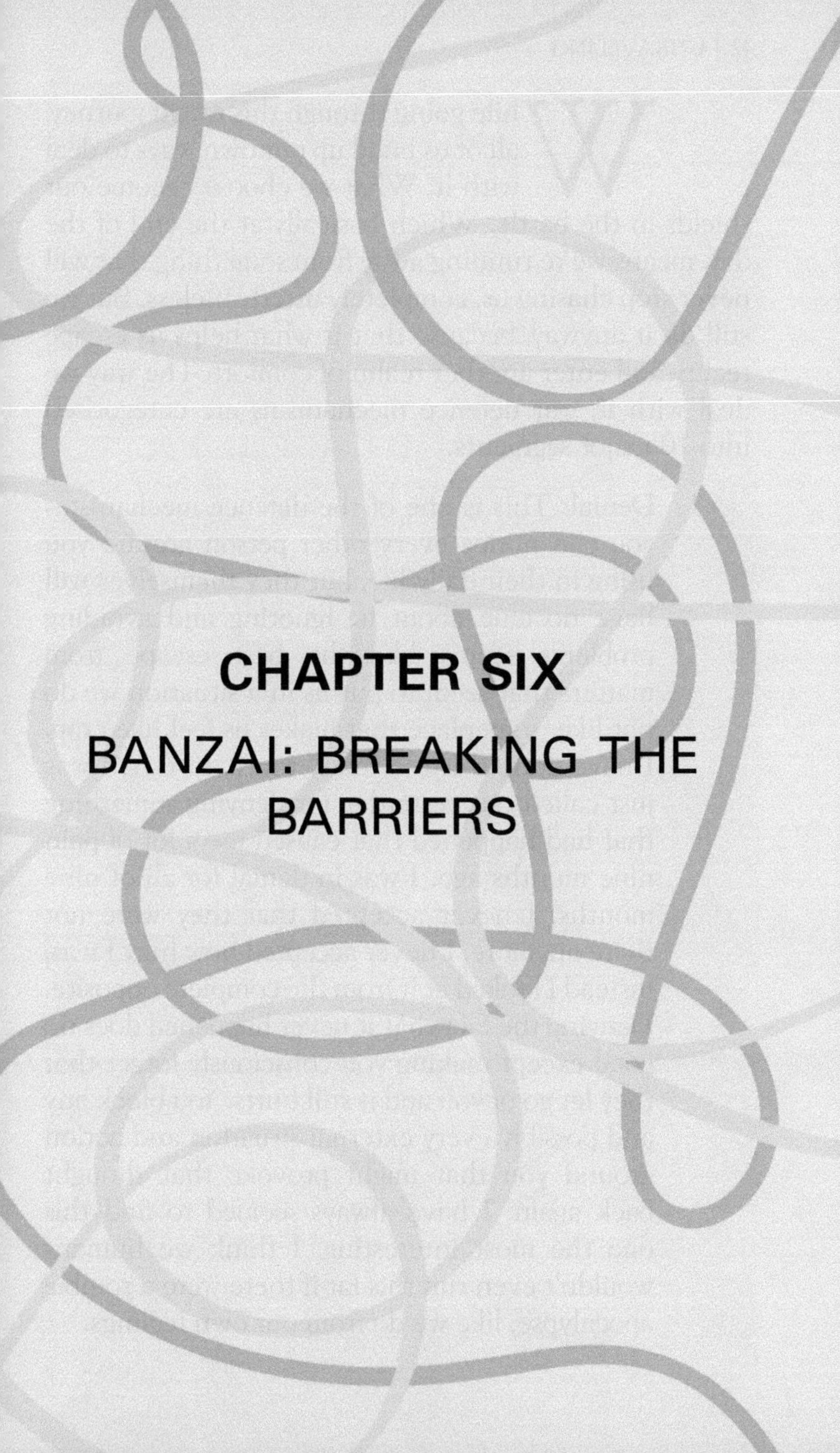

CHAPTER SIX

BANZAI: BREAKING THE BARRIERS

While going through this tough journey, all of us build up our own ways to deal with it. What we choose become our shields in the battle. Which basically at the end of the day, means we're running away from something that will never stop chasing us, completely utterly useless. But we still do it anyway, because that is what helps us escape reality and enter another realm of comfort. The way we deal with it, our defence mechanisms are categorised into 10 major segments.

1. Denial: This is one of the defence mechanisms you can notice every other person around you using in their daily life, but they themselves will have no clue about it. Ignoring and avoiding problems seems like the best escape from matters that seem to put us in a situation we do not like, someplace that makes us feel like crap. I have done this too many times, in fact, I was just called out yesterday for denying something that had happened that caused me a lot of pain nine months ago. I was in denial for all of nine months, I never accepted that they were not there anymore, I never accepted how hurt I was, instead I looked at it from the complete opposite. Denying the fact that it never happened does no good except making you consciously forget that they let go of you and it still hurts. You block any and possibly every external situation and action around you that might provoke that thought back again. I have always seemed to find this one the most interesting. I think we humans wouldn't even run this far if there were a zombie apocalypse, like we do from our own feelings.

2. Repression: Repression unlike denial is unconscious. It is unconsciously burying something that has caused you immense pain, such as the death of a closed one when it might have happened right in front of you. That is the kind of pain that can drain anyone down, and unconsciously burying it somewhere deep so you never have to feel the pain or remember the event is repression.

3. Projection: Projection is when you take their actions to highlight what you feel. When you are not ready to accept your feelings toward them, so you make yourself believe it's reciprocated. When I don't want to talk to someone and I don't admit that, I take it in a way that I make myself believe it is them who don't want to talk to me. This is something that one completely makes up in their mind; a scenario that isn't even true.

4. Displacement: Displacement is when you pour your feelings out on someone or something that shouldn't be put to blame. When you're feeling frustrated and hurt because someone left you and you go and punch some concrete walls, what's that going to do? Is it the wall's fault that that person decided to leave you? I think not. Is it that worker's fault, the one you just screamed at for no good reason? No. The displacement of feelings and emotion onto something or someone impeachable is a defence mechanism that all of us use almost every day of our lives.

5. Regression: Regression is when an adult uses childish tactics to get away from things that

bother them, such as crying or throwing a tantrum. Such as demanding a nap time for high schoolers (on that note, we do need nap time). In the adult world, things can no longer be as carefree and easy-going, but regression is escaping that world and moving steps back into childhood behaviours.

6. Rationalisation: Rationalisation is the defence mechanism that as given by its name uses logic, something that can be rationalised. We use this usually when we are wrong, and we want to prove that we are right. Stealing cash from your brother's wallet for 20 different socks and then saying it was for an assignment, and it's okay to spend money on assignments is rationalisation. It wasn't me who bought those socks by the way.

7. Sublimation: Sublimation is putting your pain and energy into something useful. Exactly what I am doing, I am writing this book as a process of sublimation. You may have taken up karate, and directed your attention there. This is one of the good defence mechanisms we use.

8. Reaction formation: Reaction formation is based on the feelings of someone against their actions. If someone is feeling drained, however, their actions of constantly smiling and laughing say the complete opposite. We often use this to clearly cover up our feelings about matters.

9. Compartmentalisation: This is when one starts dividing up their work and responsibilities into definite sections. When someone wants

to separate their work ethics from their family behaviours.

10. Intellectualisation: Intellectualisation is a defence mechanism that I personally use whenever any stressful situation comes ahead, such as letting go. I start researching in detail, about every little thing relating to the topic that causes me stress, in this way I do not allow myself to let go of it; I keep holding on.

After reading all of these defence mechanisms, you might have been able to relate to at least one, or possibly more than one. Many of these defence mechanisms unplug us from reality and put us in a world of immense comfort. But that is what we do, it is natural for all of us. It is also an important stage in development. Because these are controlled by our id and superego, there's nothing we can possibly do to erase it, we can just make it better as we go along. These are techniques we not only use while letting go but whenever we come across something we consider to be a failure. What is it that we have failed at while letting go? It is different for everyone. While something is lost, we have failed at being responsible, why does it affect me? Because being responsible was something I valued and cared about. Just like that we consider our failures to be relationships that didn't work out, hobbies that didn't work out, things that we lost, the list goes on and on. It is what we have considered being our failures. And that is what we need to accept. Not everything will go right, not every relationship is meant to work out. We simply need to accept.

WHAT I GOT FROM THIS CHAPTER

CHAPTER SEVEN

WHEN I TELL YOU

To give up is to let go. Giving up the idea, the thought that you have everything under control. Giving up that you can change everything, to make the world a better place. Giving up on the mere idea that everything has to be changed for it to be good. Giving up the idea that you can have a great life with no pain and suffering. Giving up attachment. Giving up the certainty you hold for the future. Giving up that you are always right no matter the situation. Giving up everything you're holding on to. All of these things, one by one through the process of letting go have to be given up. If I do not, then I'd still be holding on to the expectation of even the slightest change happening that will make things better sometimes, but actually, almost always nothing like that happens. Embrace what you're going through. Don't let that one expectation you've created let you stay exactly where you are, and if you don't let go and give up, this is exactly where you will be in 5 years.

What has happened in the past is something that we cannot deal with, something that we have lost control over but what happens now is something we can deal with, something we can control. The past is something that has gone away with time, something that has already happened, something that is not reality anymore. It is a concept that cannot be replayed again, except in memories. And we are the ones who control our memories. If we never keep bringing those memories back up again, the past remains a concept and not reality. You are reliving those memories to make yourself believe that the past is real. It's not. It's gone. They are gone. It is gone. It is such a simple idea we tend to complicate.

Just let go. Just let it go. Just like when you were a child and you let go of any possible matter that came along after a good cry. Holding on to things and people in the past is something we as humans have adapted and learned while growing up, something I made myself believe is important. Right now is all that counts, one day this will be in the past too. Something that will be a concept, not a reality. And this won't matter either. Very little actually matters. And all of that that matters is in the present.

All of this, all that you got from this book, all that I've written down is an illusion until you put it into action. When I'm telling other people about letting go, I am just making myself confirm that I have made any progress throughout this time. I make myself believe that now I have come up to a point where I can advise others, making myself believe that I have achieved exactly what I was looking for. Forasmuch I haven't even put any of this into action myself. If I had let go of that person, that thing that happened a year ago, if I would've just freed myself maybe then I could've actually suffered less and maybe I wouldn't be writing this. A good and a bad. But now I write this, for it to be printed and as a remembrance for me, and as an advice to you.

Today is the day I let go of you, you the thing I was holding onto, the day I free myself from the burden of the past. Thank you for all that you taught me. And thank you reader, for reading this far.

WHAT I GOT FROM THIS CHAPTER

ACKNOWLEDGMENTS

To Mom, Dad, the Patel family. To my dearest friends whose names I might regret later on if I put it here, and to the most precious pieces of my heart: my sisters and brothers. I am out of words to say how grateful and thankful I am for each one of you.

To Dr Vinod Goyal, Dr Jitesh Bhatt, Dr. Nisha Prajapati Patel, and Dr Yatin Bhushan without whom this book would've simply made no sense. Thank you.

To my supervisor, Ms Ruth Marie who believed in me, thank you for being my rock.

My biggest thank you to the ones who affected me so greatly that I was able to write something like this.

9 789354 274985

Printed by Libri Plureos GmbH in Hamburg,
Germany